ATLANTIC OCEAN

THE CARIBBEAN

TURKS AND
CAICOS ISLANDS

HAITI

DOMINICAN
REPUBLIC

PUERTO RICO

VIRGIN ISLANDS

ST. CROIX

ST. KITTS

ANTIGUA

GUADELOUPE

DOMINICA

MARTINIQUE

ST. LUCIA

BARBADOS

GRENADA

TRINIDAD
AND TOBAGO

GUYANA

VENEZUELA

ARUBA

LESSER ANTILLES

L L E S

RAIN FOREST

For Kalera,
and all you little rhyme-lovers out there

J.A. and G.N.

For Antwoin and Takysha,
and for Jane with all her patience

C.J.

Text copyright © 1991 by John Agard and Grace Nichols
Illustrations copyright © 1995 by Cynthia Jabar

First U.S. edition 1995

Library of Congress Cataloging-in-Publication Data

Agard, John, 1949–
No hickory no dickory no dock: Caribbean nursery rhymes /
written and remembered by John Agard and Grace Nichols;
illustrated by Cynthia Jabar. — 1st U.S. ed.
Summary: A collection of rhymes, both original and traditional,
that evoke the rhythms and language of the Caribbean.
ISBN 1-56402-156-4
1. Children's poetry, Caribbean (English) 2. Caribbean Area —
Juvenile poetry. 3. Nursery rhymes. [1. Caribbean Area — Poetry.
2. Caribbean poetry (English) 3. Nursery rhymes.]
1. Nichols, Grace, 1950– . II. Jabar, Cynthia, ill. III. Title.
PR9320.9.A3N6   1995
811—dc20   93-24289

2 4 6 8 10 9 7 5 3 1

Printed in Italy

The pictures in this book were done on scratchboard.

Candlewick Press
2067 Massachusetts Avenue
Cambridge, Massachusetts 02140

CARIBBEAN NURSERY RHYMES

No Hickory
No Dickory
No Dock

Written and remembered by
John Agard and Grace Nichols

Illustrated by
Cynthia Jabar

CANDLEWICK PRESS
CAMBRIDGE, MASSACHUSETTS

Authors' Note

Nursery rhymes are a timeless and unforgettable part of childhood. In this collection Humpty Dumpty mingles with Mary-Anne Marley and Doctor-Kill-And-Can't-Cure, characters inspired by the Caribbean folk tradition. Storytelling nights all around the Caribbean brought the irrepressible Anancy, the trickster spider man who, like Brer Rabbit, has his roots in Africa; and in Guyana, where we grew up, there were characters such as Mama-Wata, the mermaid of our hinterland rivers.

The influences of the English nursery rhymes cannot be forgotten. Nor can the influences of the oral Caribbean rhymes we chanted as children to the clapping of hands and skipping and ring games. We took great pleasure in drawing upon these different streams of our childhoods and riding their different rhythms.

We hope you have fun reading the poems, or better yet, saying them aloud.

—*John Agard and Grace Nichols*

Give Me Five

Give me five fingers of joy,
Give me five fingers of joy,
Give me five fingers of joy,
From every jumping girl and boy.

Give me five fingers of love,
Give me five fingers of love,
Give me five fingers of love,
From the side below and above.

Give me five fingers of play,
Give me five fingers of play,
Give me five fingers of play,
I tell you that will make my day.

Fingers tell a story,
Fingers tell their very own story.
O yes believe me,
O yes believe me,
Fingers tell a story,
Fingers tell their very own story.

Catch the morning with open hands,
Catch the morning with open hands,
Catch the morning with open hands,
Today we leave our fists behind.

John Agard

School Call In

Ting-a-Ling-a-Ling
School call in
Belly haul in,

Ting-a-Ling-a-Ling
School over
Belly turn over.

Traditional

One Two Anancy

ONE TWO
Anancy to you.
THREE FOUR
Never trust de score.
FIVE SIX
Always up to tricks.
SEVEN EIGHT
Can't play de game straight.
NINE TEN
Anancy, your tricky friend.

John Agard

No Hickory No Dickory No Dock

Wasn't me,
Wasn't me,
Said the little mouse.
I didn't run up no clock.

You could hickory me,
You could dickory me,
Or lock me in a dock.

I still say
I didn't run up no clock.

Was me who ran under your bed.
Was me who bit into your bread.
Was me who nibbled your cheese.

But please, please,
I didn't run up no clock.
No hickory,
No dickory,
No dock.

John Agard

Doctor Kill

Please remember when you're ill
Not to send for Doctor Kill.

If you have the mumps he'll give you more
        bumps.

If you have a sore he'll give you some more.

Never take a pill from this Doctor Kill
And better don't touch the medicine he pour,
For his full name is
        Doctor-Kill-And-Can't-Cure,
None other than
        Doctor-Kill-And-Can't-Cure.

Doctor-Kill-And-Can't-Cure,
Please stay away from my door.

John Agard

Granny

It so nice to have a Granny
When you've had it from yuh Mammy
And you feeling down and dammy.

It so nice to have a Granny
When she brings you bread and jammy
And says, "Tell it all to Granny."

Grace Nichols

This Old Lady from Caribee

A certain old lady from Caribee
Loved the sound of kis-ka-dee-kis-kis-ka-dee.

Somewhere up in mango tree
Kis-ka-dee bird
Singing kis-ka-dee-kis-kis-ka-dee.

Every day before her morning coffee
This old lady from Caribee
Would listen for kis-ka-dee-kis-kis-ka-dee.

Kis-ka-dee sound would start her day
And she wondered
If this was how these kis-ka-dees pray.

And as the years went by
And she could no longer see—
This old lady from Caribee

Still heard the sound of kis-ka-dee
Kis-kis-ka-dee
Kis-kis-ka-dee.

John Agard

Skipping Rope Spell

Turn rope turn, For my skipping feet. Turn rope turn, Don't trip my feet, Turn rope turn, For my feet, Turn rope turn.

Turn rope turn, Turn round and round, Turn in the air, Turn on the ground.

Turn rope turn, turn to the north, turn to the south, But please rope, please, Don't make me out.

John Agard

One for your low, Turn rope turn, Not too fast, Not too slow. One for your high,

De Bottleman

"Bottles! Bottles! Bottles I buy."
Hear de bottleman cry:

"Long bottles, short bottles,
Fat bottles, thin bottles.

Bottles! Bottles! Bottles I buy."
Hear de bottleman cry:

"Search low, search high.
I buy dem wet, I buy dem dry."

Run with a bottle to de bottleman cart
When yuh hear de bottleman cry:

"Bottles! Bottles!
Bottles I buy."

John Agard

Old Mister Goswell

Old Mister Goswell
Going to de well
Didn't like pinedrink,
Coke, or sorrel.

What he liked,
And I will tell,
Was a nice cool drink
Of water from de well.

Old Mister Goswell
Going to de well
Couldn't be bothered
By de ice-cream bell.

Grace Nichols

Ten Biscuits

Ten biscuits
In a pack
Who don't want dem
Turn their back.

Back-to-back
Sago-pap
Ten biscuits
In a pack.

Traditional

Pumpkin Pumpkin

Pumpkin
Pumpkin
Where have you been?

I been to Halloween
To frighten the queen.

Pumpkin
Pumpkin
How did you do it?

With two holes for my eyes
And a light
In me head,

I frightened the queen
Right under her bed!

John Agard

Queen Foot-She-Put

She looked so tall
In the Foot-She-Put.

She looked so grand
In the Foot-She-Put.

A great-great queen
Was Foot-She-Put.

The men fell down
At the Foot-She-Put.

She gave such a cry
In the Foot-She-Put.

They stood and shook
O the Foot-She-Put.

Foot-She-Put
Foot-She-Put,

There never was a queen
Like Foot-She-Put.

Grace Nichols

So-So Joe

So-So Joe
De so-so man
Wore a so-so suit
With a so-so shoe.
So-So Joe
De so-so man
Lived in a so-so house
With a so-so view.
And when you asked
So-So Joe
De so-so man
How do you do?
So-So Joe
De so-so man
Would say to you:
Just so-so
Nothing new.

John Agard

Mosquito Mosquito

Mosquito mosquito, why do you go
    everywhere I go?
Well my child, it's blood I follow.
Mosquito mosquito, biting people, is that all
    you know?
Yes, my child, biting people is all I know.

Well mosquito, don't bite me, bite Uncle Joe.
He always boasting he sweet from head to toe.

John Agard

Don't Cry, Caterpillar

Don't cry, Caterpillar,
Caterpillar, don't cry,
You'll be a butterfly—by and by.

Caterpillar, please
Don't worry 'bout a thing.

"But," said Caterpillar,
"Will I still know myself—in wings?"

Grace Nichols

Turtle Myrtle

Turtle Myrtle
Was slow but could hurtle
As only a hurtling turtle can.

She hurtle in water,
She hurtle on sand,
She hurtle in grass,
She hurtle on land,
As only a hurtling turtle can.

"Myrtle, Myrtle," said Mother Turtle,
"Hurtle not fuh turtle, take care, Myrtle.
Yuh ain't afraid yuh brittle back buckle?"

But Turtle Myrtle would only chuckle
And show Mother Turtle another hurtle.
U Myrtle.

Grace Nichols

Ar-A-Rat

I know a rat on Ararat,
He isn't thin, he isn't fat,
Never been chased by any cat,
Not that rat on Ararat.
He's sitting high on a mountain breeze,
Never tasted any cheese,
Never chewed up any old hat,
Not that rat on Ararat.
He just sits alone on a mountain breeze,
Wonders why the trees are green,
Ponders why the ground is flat,
O that rat on Ararat.
His eyes like saucers, glow in the dark—
The last to slip from Noah's ark.

Grace Nichols

Twinkle Twinkle Firefly

Twinkle
Twinkle
Firefly
In the dark
It's you I spy.

Over the river
Over the bush

Twinkle
Twinkle
Firefly
For the traveler
Passing by.

Over the river
Over the bush

Twinkle
Twinkle
Firefly
Lend the dark
Your sparkling eye.

John Agard

What Turkey Doing?

Mosquito one
Mosquito two
Mosquito jump
In de old man shoe.

Cockroach three
Cockroach four
Cockroach dance through
A crack in de floor.

Spider five
Spider six
Spider weaving
A web of tricks.

Monkey seven
Monkey eight
Monkey playing
Pencil and slate.

Turkey nine
Turkey ten
What turkey doing
In chicken pen?

John Agard

Hippity-Hippity-Hatch

Hippity-Hippity-Hatch
My black fowl's on her patch
Keeping her eggs
All cozy and warm
Hippity-Hippity-Hatch.

Hippity-Hippity-Hatch
My black fowl's left her patch
Her chicks have all cracked
Into the world
Hippity-Hippity-Hatch.

Grace Nichols

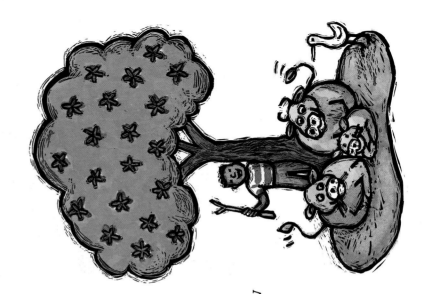

Cow Chat

Mama Moo
Papa Moo
Baby Moo
Lying in the grass,

Said Mama Moo
To Papa Moo,
"When the grass is new
I love to chew."

"And I do too,"
Said Baby Moo.

John Agard

De Popcorn Wouldn't Pop

De popcorn wouldn't pop,
De peas wouldn't grow,
De jelly wouldn't jell,
De fowlcock wouldn't crow.

De bread wouldn't brown,
De milk wouldn't flow,
De banana wouldn't ripe,
De grass wouldn't mow.

Just can't tek it no more,
Just can't tek it no more!

Grace Nichols

Here Comes the Bride

Here comes the bride
All dressed in white
White shoes and stockings
And dirty feet inside.

Traditional

Johnny-Too-Lazy

Johnny-Too-Lazy wouldn't bathe he skin,
Johnny-Too-Lazy wouldn't shave he chin,
Johnny Too Lazy wouldn't brush he teeth,
Johnny-Too-Lazy wouldn't wipe he feet,
Johnny-Too-Lazy wouldn't comb he hair,
Johnny-Too-Lazy wouldn't take a care.

When Johnny-Too-Lazy was finally wed,
His wife had to beat him out of bed.

Grace Nichols

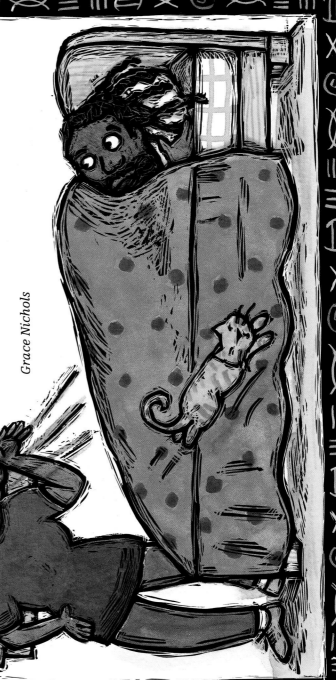

Washing-Up Day

Clothes in a tub
Rub rub rub.
Clothes in a tub
Rub rub rub.
Hand in soapy water-o
Hand in soapy water-o.

Clothes in a tub
Rub-um squeeze-um.
Clothes in a tub
Rub-um wring-um.
Hand in soapy water-o
Hand in soapy water-o.

Clothes in a tub
Come nice and clean,
But I saving up
Me money
For washing machine.

John Agard

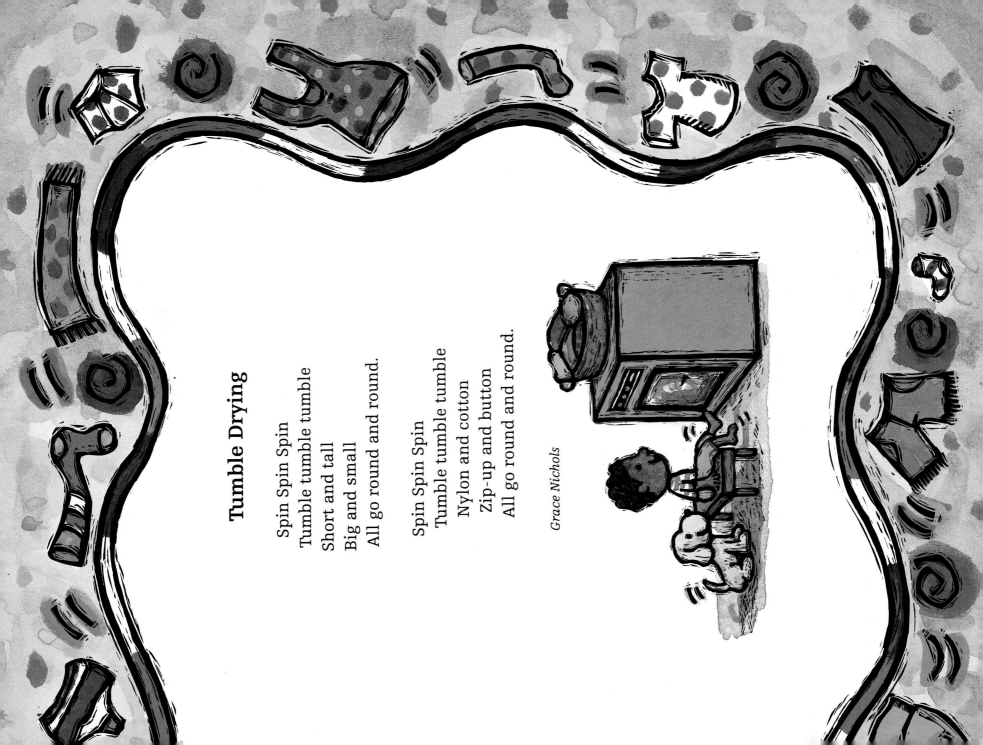

Tumble Drying

Spin Spin Spin
Tumble tumble tumble
Short and tall
Big and small
All go round and round.

Spin Spin Spin
Tumble tumble tumble
Nylon and cotton
Zip-up and button
All go round and round.

Grace Nichols

Mama-Wata

Down by the seaside
when the moon is in bloom
Sits Mama-Wata
Gazing up at the moon.

She sits as she combs
Her hair like a loom,
She sits as she croons
A sweet kind of tune.

But don't go near Mama-Wata
When the moon is in bloom,
For sure she will take you
Down to your doom.

Grace Nichols

Miss Rosie and Miss Bosie

Miss Rosie and Miss Bosie
Hanging out clothes,
Miss Rosie gave Miss Bosie
A stamp on her toes.

Next thing you know
They exchanging blows,
Miss Bosie twisting
Miss Rosie nose.

A policeman passing by
Said, "Come with me to the station,"
But they grabbed him by the collar
And called him "Botheration."

Grace Nichols

Woodpecker

Carving
tap tap
music
out of
tap tap
tree trunk
keep me
busy
whole day
tap tap
long

tap tap
pecker
birdsong
tap tap
pecker
birdsong

tree bark
is tap tap
drumskin
fo me beak
I keep
tap tap
rhythm
fo forest
heartbeat

tap tap
chisel beak
long
tap tap
honey leak
song
pecker tap
tapper peck
pecker
birdsong

John Agard

Mary-Anne Marley

Mary-Anne Marley she wouldn't marry,
Mary-Anne Marley she made her poopa angry,
Mary-Anne Marley she shook her head,
Mary-Anne Marley she sang instead:

Before me marry
Me go hug-up mango tree
Hug-up mango tree.
Before me marry
Me go hug-up mango tree
Me go live like free-bee.

A rich-rich mister he came for to marry her,
A rich-rich mister he came for to marry her,
Mary-Anne Marley she shook her head,
Mary-Anne Marley she sang instead:

Before me marry
Me go hug-up mango tree
Hug-up mango tree.
Before me marry
Me go hug-up mango tree
Me go live like free-bee.

Grace Nichols

Humpty

Humpty Dumpty did sit on a wall,
Humpty Dumpty did have a great fall.
All the king's horses and all the king's men
Did try to put him together again.

But after they left
And poor Humpty had wept,
Along came little Hugh
Who knew of super glue.

It took him a while
But Humpty Dumpty was back in style
(Now Humpty's planning to run "The Mile").
All because of little Hugh
Who fixed him up with super glue.

Grace Nichols

Pussy in de Moonlight

Pussy in de moonlight
Pussy in de zoo
Pussy never come home
Till half past two.

Traditional

London Bridge

London bridge is broken down,
Broken down, broken down.
London bridge is broken down,
My fair lady.

See de robbers passing by,
Passing by, passing by.
See de robbers passing by,
My fair lady.

What dis poor robber do,
Robber do, robber do?
What dis poor robber do,
My fair lady?

He broke my lock and stole my gold,
Stole my gold, stole my gold.
He broke my lock and stole my gold,
My fair lady.

How many pounds will set him free,
Set him free, set him free?
How many pounds will set him free,
My fair lady?

Ten thousand pounds will set him free,
Set him free, set him free.
Ten thousand pounds will set him free,
My fair lady.

Ten thousand pounds is far too much,
Far too much, far too much.
Ten thousand pounds is far too much,
My fair lady.

Then off to prison we must go,
We must go, we must go.
Then off to prison we must go,
My fair lady.

Traditional

Who Is de Girl?

Who is de girl dat kick de ball
Then jump for it over de wall?

Sally-Ann is a girl so full-o-zest,
Sally-Ann is a girl dat just can't rest.

Who is de girl dat pull de hair
Of de bully and make him scare?

Sally-Ann is a girl so full-o-zest,
Sally-Ann is a girl dat just can't rest.

Who is de girl dat bruise she knee
When she fall from de mango tree?

Sally-Ann is a girl so full-o-zest,
Sally-Ann is a girl dat just can't rest.

Who is de girl dat set de pace
When boys and girls dem start to race?

Sally-Ann is a girl so full-o-zest,
Sally-Ann is a girl dat just can't rest.

John Agard

Sir Garfield

Sir Garfield was his name
And cricket was his game.

A bat he loved to wield
A ball he loved to swing.
See Sir Garfield
On a cricket field,
And man, you see a king.

He hit one six
And he hit two six,
He hit three six
And he hit four six,
He hit five six
And he hit six six,

Six six in a row.
Licks-o licks-o!

John Agard

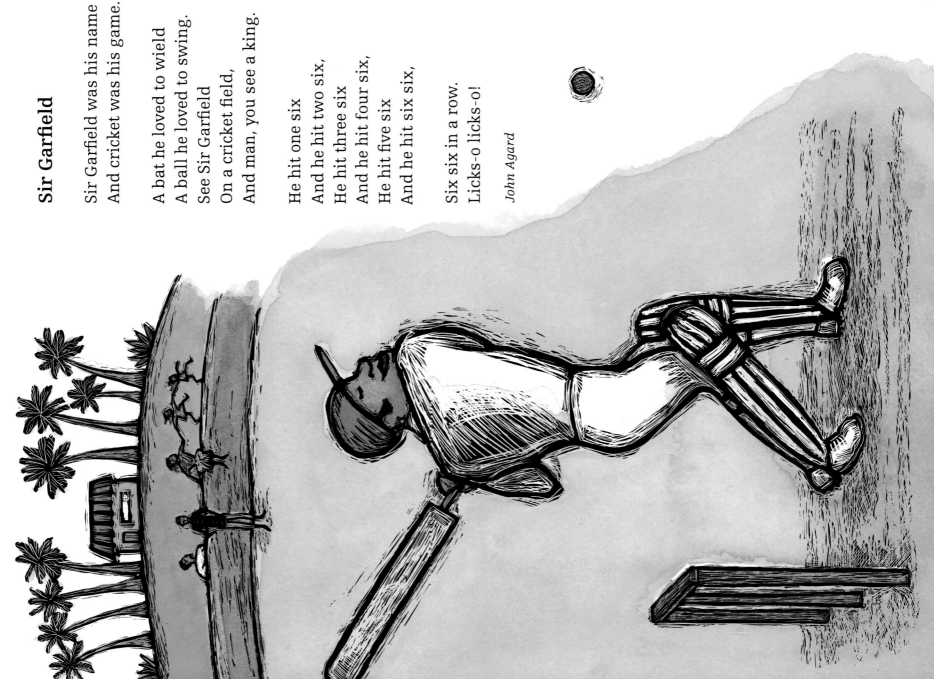

Sugarcake Bubble

Sugarcake, sugarcake
Bubbling in a pot,
Bubble, bubble sugarcake
Bubble thick and hot.

Sugarcake, sugarcake
Spice and coconut,
Sweet and sticky
Brown and gooey,

I could eat the lot.

Grace Nichols

No More Latin

*(Chanted by Children When
School Is Closing)*

No more Latin
No more French
No more sitting
On de old school bench.

No more licks
To make me cry
No more eyewater
To come out my eye.

Traditional

Baby-K Rap Rhyme

My name is Baby-K
An dis is my rhyme.
Sit back folks
While I rap my mind:

Ah rocking with my homegirl,
My mommy.
Ah rocking with my homeboy,
My daddy,
My big sister, Les, an
My granny.
Hey dere people—my posse,
I'm the business,
The ruler of the nursery.

poop po-doop
poop-poop po-doop
poop po-doop
poop-poop po-doop

Well, ah soaking up de rhythm,
Ah drinking up my tea,
Ah bouncing an ah rocking
On my mommy knee,
So happy man so happy.

poop po-doop
poop-poop po-doop
poop po-doop
poop-poop po-doop

Wish my rhyme wasn't hard,
Wish my rhyme wasn't rough,
But sometimes, people,
You got to be tough.
Cause dey pumping up de chickens,
Dey stumping down de trees,
Dey messing up de ozones,
Dey messing up de seas,
Baby-K say, stop dis—
please, please, please.

poop po-doop
poop-poop po-doop
poop po-doop
poop-poop po-doop

poop po-doop
poop-poop po-doop
poop po-doop
poop-poop po-doop

Now am splashing in de bath
With my rubber duck.
Who don't like dis rhyme
Kiss my baby-foot.
Babies everywhere
Join a Babyhood.

Cause dey hotting up de globe, man,
Dey hitting down de seals,
Dey killing off de ellies
For dere ivories,
Baby-K say, stop dis—
please, please, please.

poop po-doop
poop-poop po-doop
poop po-doop
poop-poop po-doop

Dis is my Baby-K rap,
But it's a kinda plea.
What kinda world
Dey going to leave fuh me?
What kinda world
Dey going to leave fuh me?

poop po-doop

Grace Nichols